The Persistence of a Bathing Suit

poems by

Cristina Trapani-Scott

Finishing Line Press
Georgetown, Kentucky

The Persistence of a Bathing Suit

Copyright © 2017 by Cristina Trapani-Scott
ISBN 978-1-63534-231-4 First Edition
All rights reserved under International and Pan-American Copyright Conventions.
No part of this book may be reproduced in any manner whatsoever without written permission from the publisher, except in the case of brief quotations embodied in critical articles and reviews.

ACKNOWLEDGMENTS

Sweet Lemons 2: International Writings with a Sicilian Accent, "Two Dimensions"
Bigger Than They Appear: An Anthology of Very Short Poems, "A Day at the Chemo Spa"
Paterson Literary Review, "Free"
Mamazine.com, "Funny Face"

Publisher: Leah Maines

Editor: Christen Kincaid

Cover Art: Paul Trapani, www.trapaniphoto.com

Author Photo: Kenneke Peck

Cover Design: Elizabeth Maines McCleavy

Printed in the USA on acid-free paper.
Order online: www.finishinglinepress.com
also available on amazon.com

Author inquiries and mail orders:
Finishing Line Press
P. O. Box 1626
Georgetown, Kentucky 40324
U. S. A.

Table of Contents

The Call 1

Two Dimensions 2

The Persistence of a Bathing Suit 3

Lost in Translation 4

A Day at the Chemo Spa 6

Free 7

Burying Worms in an Empty Lot 8

The Crossing 9

Climbing a Mountain on Horseback in July 10

Listening to Taiko on a Tuesday Evening in Ypsilanti 11

Funny Face 13

On Trying Not to Become Ice 14

Charcoal Image 15

Thursday Morning Every Six Months 16

The Anniversary of Sitting on the Deck 18

For Jay Scott

The Call

One moment splits the here
and now I stand
on the bank of a waterfall
up north like I did so many
times as a kid and all

I hear is the thunderous rush
of water, the thunderous
rush of thoughts
that spill one
atop the other as they swirl
in violent eddies
and breathing is now
something I have to actively
think about.
Instead, I think
about this river
and how impossible
it always was to catch
the crayfish that sat
so still at the bottom.
I think of the cloud
of sediment left
behind as it disappeared
backward under a rock

and now the safety of looking
back is just as murky
as what lies ahead
as through the telephone
line the crackling voice
calls my name.

Two Dimensions

What if we were paper
dolls, pictures traced
on a third grade
classroom floor,
lines drawn
sharp with a No. 2 pencil
then trimmed with imperfection?

I'd hang limp over a plastic
chair, melt into two
dimensions with my smile
drawn as a brown line,
a worm curving instead of curling…

or maybe I'd be carried
on a light wind like a leaf
skimming across pavement,
my paper self tossed about
hands over feet, over head over hands

The Persistence of a Bathing Suit

In the dressing room mirror each curve
        becomes a thick outline, a distorted filigree

of years curling in upon each other, but there is no
        place to hide and the marks on the white

wall must be some kind of tally
        of all the discarded bathing suits, all the flimsy

layers that reveal everything, the half-moon scar
        on a breast, the haunting whispers of sagging dreams.

This suit I've taken off sits in my hand now,
        a weathered shroud of moments that hang

like the clocks draped over a knotted limb
        in Dali's painting The Persistence of Memory,

but what persists now is not memory. What persists
        are the yellow and pink splashes of color

that on the rack obscured the vast
        space between before and after.

I place the bathing suit on a hook,
        let it dangle against that wall for a while

where in the mirror those patterns
        that would hide everything have to be exposed.

Lost in Translation

In an instant I am knotted
words that balance
on my father's tongue,
and I can feel
my skin become the air
one cell at a time as if
each misshapen
word of his unlocks the fragile
boundary that keeps me whole.

In Sicily, my aunt
kisses the air and I picture her
as I saw her that summer
in Trapani, with the worry
lines gathered
like a musical staff on her forehead.

Her silver hair was illuminated
by the sun as we
sat in her living
room watching Clint Eastwood voiced
over in Italian, and her hands
were clasped as if in some
kind of prayer, and they moved
with the rhythm of her words

that I could not understand.
They moved
as if that simple act
might make her words
solvent, but now they move

because she can't untangle
my father's words. She can't see
that air is just
air and that I am not dying

until my mother pulls at each
word, smooths each snarled
phrase that lies
between them.

Still, I feel myself tumbling
into the vast space
between what is and is not
understood, beyond the sunlit
walls of a Sicilian flat, beyond
the dark winter room
in Michigan, beyond that point
where words
might bring me back.

A Day at the Chemo Spa

We lean back in recliners
under warm blankets, drinking hot
cocoa as we are tethered to dangling
bags of liquid.

Conversation turns to weather,
though not whether there will be rain
or snow, but more specifically whether
we can hear snowflakes
as they land.

Free

We are free of the world!
my daughter shouts as she

leaps to catch a firefly. A light
across the street glows softly

against the dimming day. She can't
really mean free of the world, gone

from the cool grass under her feet,
gone from the quiet street

we live on? She chases fireflies,
catching them and soon all I see

of her in the darkness are shadow
limbs moving amid points of light

flashing quickly then disappearing.

Burying Worms in an Empty Lot

They buried dead worms
in vacant lots where
Queen Anne's Lace
hovered like small
clouds. They tied

twigs into crosses
because they saw
their parents
cross themselves
in swift gestures.

They performed ceremonies
with rosaries
of Cheerios strung
on yarn, small fingers
counting crusty beads of flour
and sugar. They bowed

their heads,
mumbled strings of words
about good
beginnings and sad
endings, because
that's what they thought
they understood.

Now they think they
understand the leaves
collecting in those
lots and the way they
look like palms
cupped as if seeking
answers to questions
no one thought to ask.

The Crossing

You stood at the other
end of the bridge. Cross,
you said. It's safe,
you said, and I saw how
the sun covered the water's
surface with tiny
shards of glass,
each holding all our
memories reflected
at odd angles so that
sometimes I was casting
and you were standing bewildered
half a world away.

Climbing a Mountain on Horseback in July

Her small body sways
back and forth as the horse
she rides moves slowly

up the mountainside and I breathe
deep hoping the mountain
air will make it easier

to take the space that spreads bit-by-bit
between us, but her horse is big
and the trail we follow weaves

like the lines on a graph,
like the lines that moved
up and down with the sound

of her heartbeat in those moments
before I knew her, before I knew
we would spend long days climbing

jargon that hovers now like shadows
on water. And here, on this mountain,
her horse saunters in one direction,

mine in another as we dance
a mountain tango, as we traverse up
and up, back and forth in silence,

until she crests and disappears before
I remember to say hold tight,
before I remember to tell her

that some trail horses spook easily,
but Cowboy Trey has her horse on a lead
and now I have to trust that he won't let go.

Listening to Taiko on a Tuesday Evening in Ypsilanti

On a night when the words
are no more than a whisper
and the walls feel too close
I go downtown to listen to taiko

to step out of the in-between
where past and present twist
like filaments around each
other until it's no use

trying to sort them out,
but now the drum sits high,
the air is cool, and there is nothing
between me and sound,

between me and the deep
resonance of the drummer's
grace and strength reverberating
and moving through

the swish of passing traffic,
through the space between
two buildings where a group
of women knit words

with deft hands, their lips
and fingers moving in the spaces
between drum beats, and I wonder
how I've come here to this place,

how I've spent all this time
moving in layered directions
trying to find where past
and present catch as if they

were chain-linked ends
that were always destined
to meet, but I know
that's not how things work.

I know that there is no clear
path to normal. There is only the steady
beat of the drum.

Funny Face

In the sun
with ear tilted
just so, freckles
dapple nose like
flecks of soupy mud

eyes too clear
to describe and I say
we'll be home soon

Those eyes will look
through the window
at the melting sun,

catch the rays reaching
up to hold the clouds
a little longer.

The highway stretches
like a ribbon of tape
an illusion of endlessness

like time, like when I made
you sit still in the corner

for some misdeed
and you
asked over
and over when

it would end, only five
minutes but your
legs filled with the morning's

playing yet to be done
couldn't help but wiggle
under the constraint.

On Trying Not to Become Ice

Snowflakes might fall
again and collect
like they did when they fused
into a small pellet

of ice that glowed
like the moon
against the white
light of the X-ray lamp.

All I can do now is watch
the Japanese maple,
look at the way each
leaf extends its tips

like fingers stretched
open to catch the wind.
All I can do now is turn
the heat up and hope

the leaves stay.

Charcoal Image

In one memory I sit on a stone
bench on the rocky shore
of Lake Superior tracing

my fingers on paper.
What I don't see
is my mother's hand

moving over a sketch pad
marking my image in charcoal,
my thick dark hair, my skinny
legs, my back arched,

a cresting wave folding
in fervent concentration.

Thursday Morning Every Six Months

there is nothing to do but wait
and thumb through back issues of magazines
and on this occasion the pages fall too easily
open to the centerfold where the sun
spills from an architects manicured
hallway. His wife

whose name is spelled like mine,
walks as if she's just passing through
as the photographer takes the shot,
but it's not lost on me as I sit
in this cotton gown in this waiting
room where the walls

move in waves of swirling patterns of pink
and teal that she's walked past
that camera nearly a hundred times
to get that shot or that she hates
when people put an "h" in her name
or that somewhere in that house

is a room where the real furniture sits;
a threadbare ottoman, a table
slightly warped so a piece of cardboard
must be wedged under it,

a cracked mirror. I pass my hand over the glossy
page, trying to feel the smooth walls, the warm sun,
the soft touch of a newly covered velvet chair.

It should be easy to believe now, after so many visits here,
so many hallways with architects and their families,
that results might fall easily from the technician's lips,
but the silence and the torn ottoman, the silence and the warped
table, flash with each swishing sound of my heart beat

as I wait for the technician to call my name, to tell me everything
   is fine,
while in the back room of my own mind I hear the threadbare
words, *this time.*

The Anniversary of Sitting on the Deck

Sitting on the deck alone
in the morning, leaves
hang thick over the fence.
The chair is a stiff
hand that presses
against my back as birds
on a wire
send messages in code.

I might have
learned each voice,
how much each
space between
the bursts of sound changes
its meaning, but now
the air is my mother's breath,

the birds her voice
singing as she did
when I was a young
girl and I would sit

on the top step outside
her bedroom waiting,
listening to her soft
melodies cut the morning silence.

I know now why she sang.
I know now why I long
for anniversaries such as this,

when the morning mist hangs
and I can feel each small
droplet collect on my skin.

Cristina Trapani-Scott lives in Northern Colorado. Her poems have been published in *Hip Mama Magazine, Mamazine.com, Public-Republic, The Paterson Literary Review* as well as in the anthologies *Bigger Than They Appear: An Anthology of Very Short Poems, Writers Reading at Sweatwaters,* and *More Sweet Lemons: International Writings With a Sicilian Accent.* She holds an MFA in Writing from Spalding University and currently teaches online.

www.ingramcontent.com/pod-product-compliance
Lightning Source LLC
LaVergne TN
LVHW041524070426
835507LV00013B/1810